Live a Life
Without
Fear

Rev J Martin

DEDICATION

I dedicate this book to my dad. May he rest in peace.

CONTENTS

ACKNOWLEDGMENTS

This book would not have been possible without the support and encouragement of my family, and the inspiration from my Heavenly Father.

A special thanks to: my editor; Pixal Design Studios for the design work, and Amazon for providing the digital tools by which I can get my message out into the world.

Finally, I would like to thank YOU, for buying my book, may it enlighten your life and bring you peace.

Introduction

Once a ship arrives at its destination, it drops anchor to ground itself, securing to a specific spot from which it will not move.

The anchor stabilizes the ship from the waves, tides, and various other movements of the sea. Similarly, we need an anchor when the waves of life come our way. Most people, however, are drifting aimlessly to sea, not knowing where they are going or what the next day will bring.

Most of us never reach our full potential because we settle for second best. We let fear control our lives'; we let fear restrict the options available to us. Fear can blind us. Rather than apply for the position you hesitate, you talk yourself out of it. Rather than attend the evening class, you decide not to go thinking you are too old.

Every fearful decision limits our life. It can get to the point we can become discouraged and beat ourselves up for not being good enough – thus, beginning a negative loop that replays again and again.

The only way to break the negative loop is to trust that God is by your side, He will give you the wisdom, the skills, and the knowledge to help you through. The winds, the waves, and the storms may come, but you're not worried— faith is your anchor.

You miss out on an opportunity; most people would be upset and negative. Not you. You know that God has something better lined up. You know that when one door closes, another one opens.

You go through a loss, a disappointment, a setback. Your emotions are pulling you towards discouragement, towards bitterness, towards self-pity, but you shake off the negative feelings, knowing that everything will be ok.

That is the anchor of faith pulling you back.

Or maybe your dream looks impossible every voice tells you it will not work out, forget it, you're wasting your time. But, your attitude is, "I might not see a way, but I know God has a way."

Many people want that level of faith, but unsure how to get it. Some simple changes are all that is necessary. Fear is no more powerful than faith, but when we reinforce fearful thoughts daily, saying things like, "I'm not good enough, I'm not smart enough, I'm not popular enough." They have the power to limit what we can achieve.

Strengthen your faith today and maintain stability during any waves of worry, doubt or fear that may toss you around. Learn to remain relaxed during emotional and confusing times, and strong during your weakest moments.

Where attention goes, God's energy flows.

Lost at Sea

In the book of Acts, chapter 27, Paul was on his way to Rome to stand trial before Caesar. The route they were travelling was hazardous and was usually not open in winter.

Paul advised his captors that continuing would undoubtedly lead to disaster. "Sirs." He said. "I believe there is trouble ahead if we go on— perhaps shipwreck and loss of cargo. Injuries and death." But they ignored Paul's warning.

Soon, a wind of hurricane force, called the Northeaster, swept down from the island. The ship was caught by the storm and could not head into the wind; so they gave way to it and were driven along. As they sailed, they could no longer see the sun or the stars, which was their means of navigation; they had become lost.

Many people are in storms because they make decisions they know will lead to disaster. They have no anchor of faith and take matters into their own hands. Thinking they know best.

How often have you been told not to do something but did it anyway, only for it to come back to haunt you? Knowing the consequences would be detrimental to your health, for example.

How often have you been advised to stay away from a specific person, but you didn't listen, and it led to more heartache and pain? When we make decisions based on our emotions, they are rarely the correct ones. We can say and do things we later regret.

Some of you might be on the verge of giving up because you see no way out of your storm. But, as Paul said to the men on the ship, "Do not be afraid— keep up your courage, and have faith in God.

Gale Force Winds

Occasionally, problems could try to convince us to worry, doubt or be fearful. It's important to remember these are just waves trying to pull us away from shore.

Make sure you stay anchored in faith; believing that all will work out. If you don't, you will drift into discouragement, self-pity, or bitterness.

You may still have thoughts of doubt, thoughts of worry, thoughts that it's never going to work out, but then your faith will kick in, reminding you not to panic, not to doubt, saying, "I know the answer is on the way.

Everything always works out for the best." God admires boldness and God admires holy courageous confidence. And when I say boldness I'm not talking about arrogance, I'm talking about, "I can do all things through Christ which strengthens me."

"I can do nothing without you, but I can do anything through you. It's not self-confidence; it's a confidence in God.

We're told we may never recover from our injury, we could accept it but because we're anchored in faith something in us says, "I have recovered from injuries before, I know God will give me the strength. I know healing is on the way."

Or perhaps you have a problem in a relationship; it doesn't look like it will ever get better, but you're tied to faith. Every time those negative thoughts try to pull you away, your anchor will draw you back, reminding you that communication is the key, that one heart to heart conversation will clear everything up.

My question for you today is, "do you have your anchor down? Do you have the hope, the expectancy, and the faith that you will accomplish your dreams? That you're going to receive the healing, that you are going to see your relationships restored? Or have you drifted into doubt, uncertain of your future?

Ghost on the Water

One day, Jesus told his disciples to go on ahead on the boat while He dismissed the crowd. Afterwards, He went up on the mountainside to pray. At this time, the boat was already a considerable distance from land, buffeted by the wind because the wind was against it.

Then shortly before dawn, Jesus went out to them, walking on the lake. When the disciples saw someone walking on water, they were terrified. "It's a ghost," they said and cried out in fear.

But Jesus immediately said to them: take courage it is I. Don't be afraid.

"Lord if it is you." Peter replied, "tell me to come to you." So Jesus called him. Peter then got out of the boat and walked on water towards Jesus. But when Peter felt the wind, he was afraid, and began to sink, crying out, "Lord, save me."

Immediately, Jesus reached out his hand and caught him. "You of little faith, why did you doubt?"

Like Peter, I have found that when I test my faith and try something new, initially I will fall. But I will get up, knowing that God is by my side, helping me on my way.

I would rather try and fall down, try and fall down, try and fall down before I learn than stay safe, afraid to do anything new.

There is a vast world out there with endless opportunities. Don't live a boring, safe life. With faith as your anchor, there is nothing you can't achieve.

Everyone is afraid to do certain things, but I want to encourage you to step out and follow your heart. Do what you want to do with the knowledge there is someone there to pick you up if you fall.

Anchor yourself in faith and live more boldly.

Joseph's Dream

In the book of Genesis, because of Joseph's dreams, his brothers threw him in a well, leaving him for dead. Then they sold him into slavery, resulting in Joseph ending up in prison. He could have become resentful, negative, and angry, but he kept anchored in faith.

He had good reason to be negative, to be angry, to be bitter. But his attitude was, "God you have the final say. People don't determine my destiny; a bad break can't keep me from my purpose. All the forces of darkness can't stop your plan for my life."

Joseph had the faith that his dream of holding a position of power would come true. And because faith was his anchor, he didn't stay disappointed; he was set free and put in second in command of all Egypt. Despite all that may come against you, like Joseph, if you still believe— your dreams will be fulfilled. You may be overwhelmed; the problem or obstacle might look too big. That sickness may be getting the better of you.

You could live feeling perpetually worried, but know that your faith will bring healing and restoration.

Remember that Joseph's faith took him from the pit to the palace.

When we find ourselves fearful that things will not work out. Recognize what has happened — we have pulled up our anchor. The good news is we can put it back down.

Instead of dwelling on the negative thoughts, I'll never be healthy; I'll never succeed, I'll never meet the right person. Turn it around, saying, thank you for the answers that are on the way. Thank you that healing is coming, success is coming, the right people are coming. That's how you remain anchored in faith.

Matthew 6:34

Therefore do not worry about tomorrow, for tomorrow will worry about itself. Each day has enough trouble of its own.

Doubt Your Doubts

When God appeared to Abraham, He promised him many things. One of which was the promise that Sarah would have a baby.

At 80 years old it seemed impossible. It had never happened before. Abraham could have dismissed it. I'm sure his friends put doubts in his mind saying things like, "Don't you think Sarah is too old to have a baby? He could have talked himself out of it, but as it says in Romans 4 TLB, Abraham never doubted.

He believed, for his faith and trust grew ever stronger, and he praised God for his blessing even before it happened. He was sure that God was fully able to do anything he promised. And because his faith was strong, he didn't worry about the fact he was too old to be a father. I'm sure Abraham considered it, but his belief was stronger.

We might think that our situation will not work out. But we must follow Abraham's example, and have faith and praise God for the blessing before it happens. We must learn to live with expectancy.

At nearly 100 years of age Sarah gave birth to a baby, the promise came to pass. It didn't happen overnight; it took time. They probably had plenty of times they were tempted to think, "it's never going to happen, were too old, it's been too long."

If they had no anchor of faith, they would have drifted into doubt, worry, and never saw the promise come to pass. I'm sure Abraham was so anchored in faith that when the waves of doubt came, he doubted his doubts.

So, the next time you're doing something new and the waves of doubt come your way, say, "I believe in God, and I doubt my doubts." Remember that doubt and worry are just trying to confuse us and steal our happiness.

When you're in a state of confusion, learn to stop and ignore what your brain is saying and listen to your heart. Just stop and say, "what's in my heart?" What do I believe? Not what do I think – instead, what do I believe? You may think that you're not good enough, but do you believe in your heart you're not? The voice of fear can seem louder but that's because you're not listening to the voice of faith.

Just because the promise hasn't happened yet, it doesn't mean that it will not happen. Like Joseph, you may have had bad breaks, but that doesn't mean that you will not fulfil your purpose.

Shake off the discouragement and shake off the self-pity. You were put here for a purpose; what God started He will finish.

Hebrews 10:36
You need to keep on patiently doing Gods will if you want him to do for you all that he has promised.

We all have times when we get what we want and times when we don't. Times when we have to wait, times when we have to stretch our faith just a little bit further. What helps me is the belief that God knows more than I do, and that things will work out in the end.

So whatever you are waiting for, no matter how hard it is in those testing times. Anchor yourself in faith, knowing that the road ahead will be better. We will never see the fruits of our faith unless we have patience. And patience is not just the ability to wait; it's also how we act while we are waiting.

It takes no genius to work out why we have these times of growth; all we have to do is watch how we behave during problems. Are you calm and relaxed knowing all will be ok or do you let thoughts of worry and doubt cloud your vision?

Anchor yourself to faith. Read scripture daily, walk in nature, take regular retreats, make prayer the centre part of your day and watch the difference it makes. You will be happier, calmer, and have more peace of mind.

Miracle of Faith

A few years ago, my uncle was diagnosed with a few different forms of cancer simultaneously. The news was devastating, but my uncle has powerful faith.

Unsure what to do, he prayed for a sign that all would be ok, as he didn't want to receive chemotherapy. Then, one day, his local church had a different bible on display; it was an old copy that contained many more books than today's version. The bible happened to be open at the book of Sirach; on flicking through, chapter 38 caught his attention, titled medicine and illness. A short extract below:

"Honor the doctor with the honour that is due in return for his services; for he too has been created by the Lord. Healing itself comes from the Most High, like a gift from a king."

My uncle took it, as a sign to follow his doctor's recommendation and all would be ok. From that moment he acted like the healing was on the way. He didn't say "if I'm cured," he said when I'm cured — speaking faith over his life.

On his next meeting, the doctors suggested a cutting-edge new treatment, so he went ahead. People told him not to get his hopes up. Even the doctors said not to expect much. But when the tests came back, the doctors couldn't believe how much the cancer had retreated. Like Abraham, he praised God for his blessing even before it happened. Within a few months, my uncle got the all clear and is now back to full strength.

Life lesson: Don't let other people talk you out of what God put in your heart. Don't let someone convince you, even if it's your doctor, to pull up your anchor of faith. Faith can do the impossible.

It's easy to keep our anchor down in calm waters, but when life gets rough it can be challenging, but if we pull it up we will get pulled out to sea and be at the mercy of the waves of doubt and worry.

Whatever may be happening in your life right now, anchor yourself in faith. There are brighter days and calmer waters ahead.

John 16:24
Until now you have not asked for anything in my name. Ask and you will receive and your joy will be complete.

Anchor of the Soul

When I was a young boy on holiday, I couldn't wait to get into the sea and play. My family would pick a place on the beach, and then we would have fun in the water.

In a couple of hours, when we were ready to take a break we would look up and realise our towels, and clothes were a few hundred yards away. We didn't recognize it, but the whole time, we had been slowly drifting.

The scripture describes faith as the anchor of the soul. It wouldn't use the word anchor unless there was a possibility of drifting. And this is what can happen in life if we don't keep our anchor down; little by little, we will start drifting. Getting a little negative, worried, and discouraged. Saying things like, "I'm never going to lose weight, I'm never going to overcome this challenge. I'm too old to change." If you think these thoughts, it means you don't have your anchor down.

You may not see how it is possible to achieve your dream but don't give up; God always rewards faith.

When you anchor yourself in faith, it doesn't mean you won't have difficulties; it means you won't drift. Nothing will move you. The storms, the waves, the tides may come, but your faith is in the Lord.

What's interesting is when I was at the beach, it wasn't a massive wave that caused us to drift it wasn't strong winds. It was the normal movement of the water. It's the normal currents of life that will pull you off course.

Perhaps you don't even realise you have drifted into doubt, but you don't believe in your dreams anymore. What used to excite you no longer does; you have lost your passion. You used to be loving, kind, and fun, but because of a setback or betrayal doubt has made you cold, dreary, and hard to get along with.

Or maybe you have drifted into worry, you used to believe that God was in control, that He took care of everything, but you pulled up your anchor of faith, now your living stressed and depressed thinking you must do everything on your strength.

If you have drifted into negativity, if you feel discouraged, if you have let thoughts of worry or doubt consume you, put your anchor down today, start believing, start expecting, and start moving towards your destiny. Life is too short to go through it drifting—negative, worried, with no faith in your abilities. Plus, when we don't have faith, it limits what God can do.

That's why Paul told Timothy, "Stir up your gifts." We must stir up our faith; otherwise, we will drift.

Some people's view is, well, if God is so good why haven't my dreams come to pass? Why did I have these bad breaks? Well, it's because an enemy of your soul is trying to keep you from your destiny.

That voice that whispers in your ear, "you're not good enough, you're not smart enough, you will never fulfil your dreams. That person hurt you, you have a right to be bitter."

The only way to quieten that voice is to speak words of faith over your life. When you have thoughts of doubt worry or judgement speak positive loving and encouraging words. When we speak words of faith on a daily basis, those words fill us with the Holy Spirit, and there is no space left for negativity.

James 3:5
Likewise, the tongue is a small part of the body, but it makes great boasts. Consider what a great forest is set on fire by a small spark.

Cut Those Lines

A man was visiting the Zoo one day when he noticed the only thing holding the elephants was a small rope tied to their front leg: no chains, no harness, no cages. It was clear the elephants could, at any time, break free from the ropes but they did not.

When the man saw a trainer, he asked him why the magnificent animals just stood there and did not try to get away. "Well, when they're much smaller we use the same size of rope to tie them and, at a young age, it's enough to hold them. Then as the calves grow up, they're conditioned to believe they cannot break away. They believe the rope can still hold them, so never try to break free."

The man was amazed. These powerful animals could break free at any time, but because they believed they couldn't, they were stuck.

The elephants had become so accustomed to being held back by the rope, that the line itself was enough to keep them in check. If only the elephants knew how strong they were. If only they realized that the rope could no longer contain them. Then they would be free. But they don't.

Worry and doubt are like that rope; from an early age, they have a hold of us. It can feel like we are tied and unable to escape. The truth is, fear has no power over us only the power we give it. We fail to see our real strength. At any moment we can pull away into faith, and live life as God intended.

Just as we have been conditioned to worry and doubt, it will take conditioning to break away and become anchored in faith. Daily prayer and devotion is a great starting point.

Gone Fishing

Two of my friends love to fish and often rent a boat. Once, they sailed out into the sea for about an hour to find deep waters and fished there for most of the morning.

When they were ready to return, Seamus asked Chris to pull up the anchor. He pulled and pulled with all his strength, but it was stuck. Seamus then came, and both pulled, but it still wouldn't move. So, Chris cranked up the engine and started to pull away; hoping he could dislodge the anchor, but it must have been caught under a big rock because when he pulled forward, the anchor pulled the boat backwards.

Then he circled and tried to pull in different directions, but his efforts were in vain, it wouldn't come loose. Finally, Seamus took out his Swiss army knife and cut the line, leaving the anchor there in the ocean.

Sometimes, we too can be anchored in the wrong things, and they don't come off easily. Maybe you're always judging yourself, judging every move you make. "I shouldn't have done that; I shouldn't have said that. Why did I eat that, why did I not stand up for myself."

All you can do is your best and know that God understands and sees your heart. Stop trying to impress yourself and others. Saying, "I'm not where I want to be, but at least I'm not where I used to be.

If you have been anchored in doubt, fear, or worry for a long time, like my friend, to break free you need to cut those lines. The enemy doesn't want you to be free. He doesn't want you to be anchored in faith; he wants you to be worried, angry, bitter, and depressed.

It's time to say, "I've been anchored in negativity long enough. I'm tired of living depressed and worried. I'm cutting those lines today." I'm anchoring myself in faith.

When we have the right perspective, that setback will be temporary. That lay off will be a new beginning. That dark cloud will have a silver lining. We may have disappointments, but we know they cannot stop our destiny. When you stay anchored in faith, you will excel in life in ways you cannot imagine.

Life Without Limbs

Nick Vujicic was born without arms or legs. He had a hard time at school, as he couldn't play sports like the rest of the children or run in the playground.

Growing up, Nick had very few opportunities, but the one thing he had was loving, supportive parents who encouraged him and told him he was beautiful just the way he was.

All Nick wanted was hope and happiness but failed to see it for many years. Throughout his childhood, he struggled with depression and loneliness, always wondering why he differed from all the other children. He even questioned the purpose of his life, or if he even had a purpose? Nick could have been angry and bitter, saying, God, why did this happen but he kept anchored in faith.

Then, one day reading the Bible he got his answer in John chapter 9 when he learned about Jesus and the blind man. The disciples asked Jesus, "why was this man born blind. Was it the result of his sins or the sins of his parents?"

"Neither this man nor his parents sinned," said Jesus, "but this happened so the works of God might be displayed in him."

Nick thought if God had a plan for the blind man then he had a plan for him. So, rather than compare himself to others he embraced his uniqueness. That moment started his relationship with Jesus. Soon, youth groups called him asking for him to share his testimony, which led to more speaking opportunities.

Since his first speaking engagement at age 19, Nick has travelled the world, sharing his story with millions and speaking to a range of diverse groups such as students, teachers, young people, and church congregations of all sizes.

What gives his message so much power is the fact that he has no limbs, people can instantly connect with his message of overcoming adversity.

Today, this dynamic young evangelist has accomplished more than most people achieve in a lifetime. A bad break can't stop you. When you come up against problems, don't you dare pull up your anchor – instead, do like Nick and keep moving forward in faith. Knowing God has a plan for your life.

Are You Drifting?

If you don't stay anchored in faith, over time, you can become anchored in something else. You can become anchored in discouragement. You wake up in the morning discouraged; you work a job that makes you feel discouraged, you see everything through a tainted perspective.

I know people that are anchored in bitterness. They're so focused on their bad breaks, on the people that hurt them, that it's poisoning their life. And they may have a good reason to feel that way I'm simply saying staying anchored in those things will keep them from their destiny. It will cause them to miss their purpose.

If you are anchored in something that is holding you back, it's time to cut those lines and come over into faith. God didn't create you so you could go around anchored in bitterness, anchored in doubt and worry. He created you to be anchored in faith.

Go out each day with expectancy, knowing that the days ahead are more significant than the days past. And if you face difficulties, have the right perspective.

If David had looked at Goliath and thought, "I'll never defeat him, he's twice my size— I don't stand a chance." Had David been anchored in doubt, we would not be talking about him today. The problems that come our way are not meant to stop us; they are intended to develop our character, they're expected to move us towards our divine destiny.

Instead of being negative, saying things like, "why is this happening to me, why do things always go wrong? When are things ever going to work out?" Turn it around by saying, "Lord, I don't see a way, but my faith is in you. I know you have a way; I know you will get me to where I'm supposed to be."

In James Gospel, it says, "you must believe and not doubt, because the one who doubts is like a wave of the sea, blown and tossed by the wind."

If you don't have the faith that the problem will turn around, that the healing is on the way, that the new job is in your future. You will have a negative feeling about life; frustrated and stressed most of the time.

We all go through seasons where it's not exciting; it's so easy to lose our enthusiasm. Those are the average currents of life. Nobody is happy all the time.

It's easy to have faith in the summer times of life when all is going to plan, and the sun is in the sky. It's when winter kicks in. Those dark, fearful nights can take their toll. When nothing seems to change when what we want is taking longer than expected. In the bad times, it's so important to keep a smile on our face, to live with expectancy, saying, "thank you Lord that something good is on the way.

Some people will say; what if I do that and nothing happens?

What I have found is, when you believe good things are on the way, you see the world differently. You look at the silver lining. You focus more on the good than the bad.

When we have thoughts of doubt, worry or fear the best way to overcome them is to open our mouth and speak words of faith. "I can't do that." No. "With God's help, I can do anything. I'm going to move forward in faith." I would rather go through life anchored in faith than anchored in fear, worry, or doubt. That will only draw in more negativity.

Waiting Room

Doubt and unbelief come when we are waiting. If we prayed and got what we wanted immediately, we would never have a problem. So why does God make us wait? Our faith must be tested for us to grow. It must be strong enough to handle the next level of our destiny. When you stretch your faith, it causes growth.

Most of you today might feel like you're being stretched. In your work life, family life, or social life. But it all depends on how you look at stretching. If you look at it negatively, it will affect you emotionally and physically. But if you look at it as growth, as something you must go through, to make you stronger and wiser— you will look at it differently.

It's important to understand that God can change your life in a second. If your life is not going as planned, you have to ask yourself, are you holding onto any un-forgiveness, guilt or regret?

You must release those things to transcend to the next level of your destiny.

Calm the Storms of Life

One day, as evening came, Jesus said to his disciples, "Let us go over to the other side of the lake." So, they took the boat leaving the crowd behind.

As they moved out into the middle of the lake, a furious squall came up, and the waves broke over the boat, so it was nearly swamped. Jesus was in the stern, sleeping on a cushion. The disciples woke him and said, "Teacher, don't you care if we drown?"

He got up, rebuked the wind and said to the waves, "Quiet! Be still!" The moment He spoke, the winds started to die down, and soon it was completely calm.

Then He said to his disciples, "Why are you so afraid? Do you still have no faith?"

They were terrified and asked each other, "Who is this? Even the wind and the waves obey him!"

Like the storm In this story, the storms of life can come upon us in the same way, quickly and unexpectedly. For some of us, life can seem like one storm after another. We wake up in a storm, go to work; there's a storm, come home, and our family life is in a storm. Diagnosis of illness can cause a physical, mental, or emotional storm.

Reading the word of God, it's clear that the storms of life are inevitable, but it's how we handle them that determines our destiny. Will they beat us or will we look to Jesus for help, and grow through them?

A ship survives a storm by letting down its anchor on a firm foundation. When the winds and waves of life threaten to carry us out to sea, the best security we have is dropping our anchor of faith.

Many people put their anchor in their career, possessions, or social status, and for a time that can make them feel secure. Then a storm comes, and they feel stranded, not knowing what way to turn. However, when you anchor yourself in faith, Jesus will give you the peace within your heart to do what is right, He can calm the storms in your life.

Free as a Bird

A man once bought a small bird and placed it in a cage. "Give me my freedom, "cried the little bird. Shocked that the bird talked to him, the man listened to see if it would say anything else.

"I am of no use to you sir, I have no beautiful feathers nor can I sing, and I'm far too small to eat. However, if you promise to grant me my freedom, I will tell you three wise teachings."

The man agreed, at which point the little bird told him: "First: Do not be upset about things that have already happened. Second: Do not wish for what is unattainable. Third: Do not let greed blind you from the truth."

"Indeed," the man said. "These are wise teachings." So as agreed, he set the little bird free. The man sat and pondered on what the bird had said. Meanwhile, the bird flew up to a branch high in a tree.

Then the man heard the bird laughing. "Why do you laugh?" he called.

"I'm laughing because I so easily won my freedom," replied the bird. "I'm only a little bird yet I have made a fool out of you. Within me lies a diamond the size of a duck egg. You missed out on being a wealthy man."

On hearing the news, the man became depressed, sad and angry. In his anger, he tried to recapture the bird but to no avail.

When the man had worked himself out the little bird flew to a lower branch and called out. "You granted me my freedom because I gave you three teachings, yet you instantly forgot them."

You should not be upset over things that have happened, but still, you're upset that you set me free. You should not wish for the unattainable, and yet you want me, a bird, to come down and enter a prison. You should not let greed blind you from the truth, yet you think that I have a diamond the size of a duck egg inside my tiny body." With that, the little bird flew away.

Like the man in this story, how often have you been told wise teachings but instantly forgot them; you may hear but do you listen?

Often, we get so wrapped up in our emotions we lose sight of the truth. We can take a lot of stress and worry on our shoulders, thinking we must do everything on our strength. Part of faith is trust. We must trust in the Lord and not lean on our own understanding; we must believe that all will work out to His plan.

Look back on your life, remember the problems that were once mountains are now molehills. If worrying and doubting didn't work in the past, why would they work now?

Wisdom is the ability to apply experience so as not to make the same mistakes again. When you anchor yourself in faith, it allows God's power to work in your life. It will give you the wisdom to sit down with a loved one rather than let the relationship fall apart. The wisdom that no amount of self-improvement can make up for lack of self-acceptance, and that your beliefs determine your quality of life.

When you anchor yourself in faith, you will apply for the new job or go for the promotion. It will give you the energy to do the things you didn't think you could. Faithful thoughts can help you see a way around even your most difficult problems.

Anchor yourself in faith, only focus on positive thoughts. Let them replay in your mind, so you don't drift into worry and doubt. Anchor yourself in faith and know your worth. Know that you're a child of God graced with unique gifts and abilities to make this world a better place.

You have been created to be of service to others. Don't be held back by fear. Put down your anchor today. Move forward with expectancy and great things will flow into your life. You will overcome every challenge, accomplish every dream and become everything you were created to be.

LET
YOUR **FAITH**
BECOME
BIGGER
THAN
YOUR FEARS.

ABOUT THE AUTHOR

I live on the northwest coast of Ireland. I use this medium to share my true voice. I wish to enlighten others and help them to see that God wants the very best for them. We often make it hard for him to enter our lives as we focus on the dark clouds rather than the silver lining.

In this growing digital frontier I just want to shed a little light out into the world to light up peoples lives in the hope that they to will help inspire others which will slowly but surely change the world, even in a small way.

My Other Books

God's Perfect Timing
The Power Of Letting Go
The Power Of Choice
The Power Of Words
Make Space for God

Printed in Great Britain
by Amazon

18433872R00027